Lisa D. Hoff

COLUMBIA

South Carolina

Self-guided Tours in 88 Pictures

COLUMBIA - Past and Present

In 1786, one hundred and sixteen years after the first English settlers arrived on their vessel Carolina and set up a small settlement on the banks of the Ashley River, the South Carolina Assembly voted to move the state capital from Charleston to a piece of land along the banks of the Congaree near the confluence of the Broad and Saluda rivers. The backcountry had been largely settled by German-Swiss Lutherans and Scotch-Irish Presbyterians who worked on family farms and did not own slaves. They felt they were not sufficiently represented and complained that law enforcement and protection were inadequate, and that they had to pay taxes to support the Anglican church to which they did not belong. The only court in the colony was in Charleston and could only be reached after an arduous and long trip.

The issue of moving the capital from the lowcountry to a new location "in the wilderness" raised concerns that the new capital would be beyond the reach of justice and become the refuge of outlaws. Senator John Lewis Gervais of Saxe-Gotha (Lexington) responded that he hoped that the oppressed of every land might find refuge "under the wings of Columbia." Columbia, the first city in the United States to bear that name, was a planned city from the beginning. The two-square-mile tract on Taylor's Hill was laid out in a grid plan with wide streets and avenues. In 1790, a constitutional convention met in the new State House and Columbia was made the permanent state capital. The same year, a regular stage line was established linking Charleston and Columbia.

Life in the little frontier town was simple and quiet, with an occasional horse race and social, religious and civic assemblies. Sessions of the legislature which met for several weeks every December provided the most excitement. Churches and houses in the new capital were simple wooden structures, but the town's first newspaper, the Columbia Gazette, appeared in 1791 and its first grammar school, the Columbia Academy, opened its doors in 1797. In 1805, South Carolina College, now the University of South Carolina, was started with nine students and a faculty of two. The college and its activities played a major role in Columbia throughout the antebellum years. Commencement festivities with their academic processions, student debates and a grand ball coincided with the legislative sessions and were not to be missed.

The first half of the 19th century was a prosperous time, and Columbia soon became the trading and financial center of the state. Invention of the cotton gin made South Carolina the nation's biggest cotton exporter. With the help of canals on the Congaree, Saluda and Broad rivers, the upland or short-staple cotton arrived at the foot of Elmwood from where it was hauled to Cottontown (Main Street and Elmwood Avenue) and then on to Charleston for shipment to the mills of Great Britain and New England. With the construction of the first textile mill on the Saluda River, as well as several saw mills, cotton gins, tanneries, cooperages, carriage factories, brick kilns, iron foundries and grist mills, Columbia became a manufacturing center as well. When the state's first gas lights and a water system were installed, Columbia shed the look of a sleepy frontier town.

The favorite organized sport was horse racing. February races were the top social event of the year. Schools were dismissed, the legislature excused its members and judges adjourned the courts, and everybody flocked to the Congaree Race course between Devine Street and Millwood Avenue. At one time Columbia had seven race tracks. New railroads to Charleston, Spartanburg, Greenville, Charlotte and Savannah connected Columbia with the upcountry, the Atlantic Coast, North Carolina and Georgia.

In 1860, when Lincoln became president South Carolina called for secession from the Union. The Secession Convention opened in Columbia on December 17, 1860 at the First Baptist Church on Hampton Street. The city was thronged with politicians and visitors when smallbox broke out and the convention adjourned to Charleston. On December 20, 1860, South Carolina voted unanimously to leave the Union. The war began four months later at Fort Sumter. Although Columbia was outside the war zone for almost the entire four years of the Civil War, a military atmosphere pervaded the city. Troops were mobilized, military hospitals and prisoner-of-war camps set up, and various offices of the Confederacy established. Refugees from Charleston, Georgia and elsewhere brought the population to over 25,000. Bank monies, printing plants, rare books, valuable papers and the bells of St. Michael's Church in Charleston were brought to Columbia for safekeeping. Sherman and his soldiers arrived in Columbia on February 17, 1865. When Columbia's mayor surrendered he was assured that the citizens and their property would not be harmed. But in the evening fires started, apparently lit by drunken soldiers, and by the next morning, a thirty-six-square-block area in the heart of the city had been destroyed.

The last quarter of the 19th century saw big changes in Columbia. Electricity and telephone lines were installed, streetcars, bicycles and automobiles made the farthest places easily accessible, and the first public schools and a permanent hospital brought education and healthcare to all Columbians. A boom in textiles provided jobs in new mills and factories. The year 1896 was one of historic sports significance, Carolina and Clemson played each other for the first time at the state fairgrounds in Columbia. Carolina won 12:6.

In the years following the turn of the century the city sprawled in all directions, and through annexation of suburban areas, the population soared to almost 38,000, which did not include the 45,000 officers and enlisted men of the Thirtieth and Eighty-first Divisions who were training at the new army training facility, Camp Jackson, later to be named Fort Jackson. The Depression saw the folding of several banks, but Columbia's diversified economy, the proximity of the army training facility and the city's hundreds of employees in government and education helped cushion the shock of the Depression. When it became evident that the United States would enter World War II, Fort Jackson became America's largest training camp and South Carolina's second largest city. Today Fort Jackson is a community made up of 97,000 soldiers, civilian employees, retirees and family members. More than 67,000 soldiers train there annually. Fort Jackson was incorporated into the City of Columbia in 1968.

In 1951, Columbia received the All-American City award in recognition of its efficient operation and its adoption of a modern municipal government.

When many Deep South cities faced violence and riots during the civil rights struggles of the 1960's, Columbia's mayor, Lester Bates, called together a biracial committee of 60 businessmen to discuss the problem of racial desegregation. This group in turn selected a "secret committee" to work towards the segregation of the city. Quietly step by step the committee accomplished its goal. The University of South Carolina was desegregated in 1963, and a year later, 24 black students entered previously all-white public schools. In 1965, the city was honored with its second All-American City award for progress toward racial desegregation and involvement of black citizens in city government.

Heightened interest in the preservation of Columbia's history led to the restoration and refurbishing of many of Columbia's historic homes and to the conversion of old buildings into museums. The opening of Riverfront Park on the banks of the Old Columbia Canal in 1983 was the first step towards the goal of linking Main Street and the River through small parks, shaded pedestrian trails, residential neighborhoods, retail districts, cultural sites and the university and government offices. The Congaree Vista Project brings the 200-year old urban plans of John Gabriel Guignard with his vision of wide streets and gracefull tree-lined neighborhoods interspersed with government, education and business full circle.

Acknowledgements:

My special thanks go to Mr. and Mrs Lester Bates, Jr, whose hospitality and warm friendship have made my visits to Columbia very special.

Photo and Art Credit:

Coates Crewe, pages 36a, 44a, 53, 62
Columbia Museum of Art, page 19
Greater Columbia Convention & Visitors Bureau, page 12
Hoff Anne-Christine, page 26
Riverbanks Zoo & Garden, page 45
Security Federal Savings and Loan Association, page 9
South Carolina Division of Tourism, pages 44b, 60
South Carolina State Museum, page 37b

About the Author:

Lisa D. Hoff, a native of Austria, graduated from the University of Innsbruck with a doctorate in law. She also attended John Hopkins University and the Art Institute of Atlanta. Lisa Hoff has been a publisher, editor and photographer of the "in-88-Pictures" guide book series since the publication of the first Atlanta picture book in 1988. Her company, Cities in Color, Inc. has been responsible for providing more than 150,000 pictorial guides to sightseers in the United States and around the world.

Index

Page		
1 - 3	South Carolina State House	
	Main Street and Gervais Street	
	Tel.: 803-734-2430 (entrance from Sumter Street)	
	Hours: Mon.-Fri. 9-5, Sat. 10-5, First Sun. of Month 1-5	
	Tours: Mon.-Fri. on the hour and half hour from 9-12 & 1:30-3:30, on Sat. 10:30, 11:30, 1:30, 3:30, First Sun. 1:30 and 3:30.	
	Admission: Free	
6, 7	Trinity Episcopal Church	
	1100 Sumter Street	
	Tel.: 803-771-7300 (call for tours)	
12	Confederate Relic Room & Museum	
	920 Sumter Street	
	Tel.: 803-734-9813	
	Hours: Mon.-Fri. 8:30-5, First & Third Sat. 10-4	
	Admission: Free	
13	South Caroliniana Library	
	USC Horseshoe, 900 Block of Sumter Street	
	Tel.: 803-777-3131	
	Hours: Mon., Wed., Fri. 8:30-5, Tues. & Thur. 8:30-8, Sat. 9-1	
	Admission: Free	
14	McKissick Museum	
	USC Horseshoe, 900 Block of Sumter Street	
	Tel.: 803-777-7251	
	Hours: Mon.-Fri. 9-4, Sat. 1-5, Sun. 1-5	
	Admission: Free	
16	Longstreet Theatre	
	Greene & Sumter Streets	
	Tel.: 803-777-2551	
17	First Presbyterian Church	
	1324 Marion Street	
	Tel.: 803-799-9062	
18, 19	The Columbia Museum of Art	
	Main at Hampton Street	
	Tel.: 803-799-2810	
	Hours: Tues.-Sat. 10-5, Wed. 10-9, Sun. 1-5	
	Admission: Yes	
20	First Baptist Church	
	1306 Hampton Street	
	Tel.: 803-256-4251	
21	Seibels House	
	1601 Richland Street	
	Tel.: 803-252-7742	
23	Woodrow Wilson Boyhood Home	
	1705 Hampton Street	
	Tel.: 803-252-1770	
	Hours: Tues.-Sat. 10:15-3:15, Sun. 1:15-4:15	
	Admission: Yes (tickets available at R. Mills Hse.)	
24	Robert Mills House	
	1616 Blanding Street	
	Tel.: 803-252-1770	
	Hours: Tues.-Sat. 10:15-3:15, Sun. 1:15-4:15	
	Admission: Yes	

25	Hampton-Preston Mansion 1615 Blanding Street Tel.: 803-252-1770 Hours: Tues.-Sat. 10:15-3:15, Sun. 1:15-4:15 Admission: Yes (tickets available at R. Mills Hse.)	40, 41	Riverfront Park/Historic Canal Located off Laurel Street Tel.: 803-733-8331 Open daily 10 a.m. - 11 p.m.
28	Manns-Simons Cottage 1403 Richland Street Tel.: 803-252-1770 Hours: Tues.-Sat. 10:15-3:15, Sun. 1:15-4:15 Admission: Yes (tickets available at R. Mills Hse.)	42	The State Farmers Market Bluff Road Tel.: 803-737-4664 Mon.-Sat. 6 a.m. - 9 p.m. Tours available.
29 - 31	Governor's Green and Governor's Mansion 800 Block of Richland Street Tel.: 803-737-1709 (tours 803-737-1710) Tours of Mansion after 2001 by appointment Gift Shop open Mon.-Fri. 9:30-4:30 Admission: Free	46	Koger Center for the Arts 1051 Greene Street Tel.: 803-777-7500 Contact center for schedule of events.
		47	Richland County Public Library 1431 Assembly Street at Hampton Street Tel.: 803-799-9084 Hours: Mon.-Thurs. 9-9, Fri.,Sat. 9-6, Sun. 2-5:30
32, 33	Finlay Park 930 Laurel Street Tel.: 803-733-8331 Festivals, concerts, picnics, restaurant	51	Millwood Plantation Ruins Garner's Ferry Road Tel.: 803-252-1770 (call for reservations) Tours at 2 p.m. the last Sunday of the month.
34, 35	Riverbanks Zoo & Garden I-26 at Greystone Blvd. (500 Wildlife Pkwy.) Tel.: 803-779-8717 Hours: Daily 9-4, summer weekends 9-5 Admission: Yes	52	Fort Jackson Museum Building 4442, Jackson Boulevard Tel.: 803-751-7419 Hours: Tues.-Fri. 10-4, Sat. 1-4 Admission: Free
37	South Carolina State Museum 301 Gervais Street Tel.: 803-898-4921 Hours: Mon.-Sat. 10-5, Sun. 1-5 Admission: Yes	53	Lake Murray Tourism & Recreation Association P.O.Box 1783, Irmo, SC 29063 Visitor Center in Lorick Plantation House 2184 North Lake Drive Tel.: 803-781-5940, 800-951-4008

54 Congaree Swamp National Monument
    200 Carolina Sims Road, Hopkins, SC 29061
    Tel.: 803-776-4396
    Hours: Open daily 8:30-5
    Admission: Free

55 Historic Camden Revolutionary War Site
    includes fort sites, log cabins and the Kershaw-
    Cornwallis House
    US Hwy 521, South Camden
    Tel.: 803-432-9841
    Hours: Mon.-Sat. 10-5, Sun. 1-5
    (tours Tues., Fri., Sat., Sun.)
    Admission: Free

56 Swan Lake Iris Garden
    West Liberty Street Extension, Sumter
    Tel.: 803-778-5434, 800-688-4748
    Hours: Open daily
    Admission: Free

57 Edisto Memorial Gardens and Horne Wetlands Park
    US Hwy 301, Orangeburg
    Tel.: 803-533-6020
    Hours: Daily 8 a.m. to dusk
    Arts Center Mon.-Thurs. a.m.
    Admission: Free

58 Boone Hall Plantation
    Long Point Road, Mount Pleasant
    Tel.: 843-884-4371
    Hours: Mon.-Sat. 8:30-6:30 (winter 9-5),
    Sun. 1-5 (winter 1-4)
    Admission: Yes

59 Charleston: for details about sites please see
    Charleston in 88 Pictures by Cities in Color, Inc.
    Charleston Visitor Center
    375 Meeting Street and Ann Street
    Tel. : 843-720-5678
    Hours: Daily 8:30-5:30
    Daily admission for film.

In 1786, the General Assembly passed legislation to move the capital of South Carolina from Charleston inland to a site more centrally located. Construction of this State House was begun in 1850 and completed in 1907. The architect of the building was Viennese architect, John R. Niernsee. The exterior walls and columns are blue granite quarried and carved in Columbia. The dome is made of steel sheathed with copper.

The present building is South Carolina's third State House. The six bronze stars on the west and southwest walls mark where the building was struck by Union shells during the Civil War in February, 1865. The columns on the porticos are each carved from a single piece of stone and are believed to be the largest monolithic columns used in a building in the United States.

The main lobby of the State House connects the House Chamber (Assembly Street side) with the Senate Chamber (Sumter Street side). The stairs and balcony supports are made of cast iron, the stamped metal ceiling was installed when the dome was completed in 1902. The statue is of South Carolina statesman, John C. Calhoun. Each chamber displays portraits of notable South Carolinians.

Statue of President George Washington who visited Columbia in 1791. The walking cane was broken off by Sherman's soldiers during the occupation of Columbia.

The Confederate Monument was unveiled in 1879. This memorial to Confederate soldiers was commissioned by a Columbia ladies' group.

Statue of General Wade Hampton III, State Senator and Governor of South Carolina.

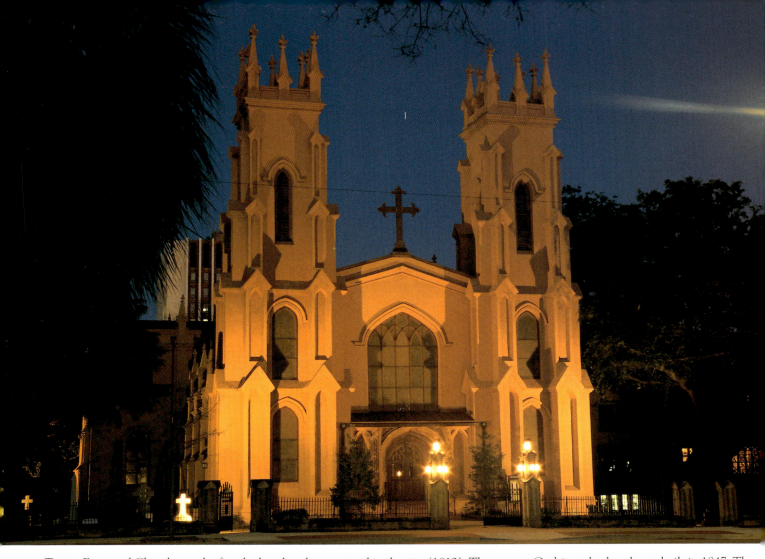

Trinity Episcopal Church was the fourth church to be organized in the city (1812). The present Gothic-style church was built in 1847. The churchyard is the last resting place for six governors, three Wade Hamptons and their families, and the poet laureate of South Carolina, Henry Timrod. The church was designated a cathedral in 1976.

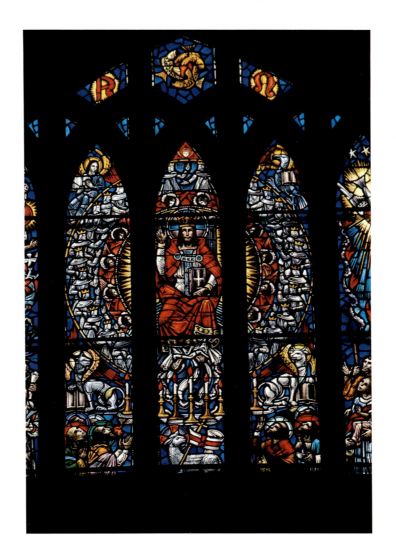
Window of Trinity Episcopal Church.

Main Street seen from the State House. Columbia was a planned city. John G. Guignard surveyed a two-mile square and laid out streets in a regular grid pattern. Assembly and State streets, named for the legislature, were to be the grand boulevards and main arteries, however, the most prestigious businesses opened on Main Street. All streets running parallel to the river were named for Revolutionary War heroes.

Main Street as seen on February 18, 1865. Two weeks after entering South Carolina, General Sherman and his troops arrived on the banks of the Congaree River and began shelling the city. Within a day, the Union Army occupied the city and began looting stores and homes. Soon drunken soldiers started fires which, fueled by high winds, raged out of control. The next morning Columbia's business district lay in ashes.

South Carolina's State Tree, the Palmetto. The Palmetto Monument (opposite page), on the grounds of the State House, was erected as a memorial to the members of the Palmetto Regiment who fell in the Mexican War of 1847.

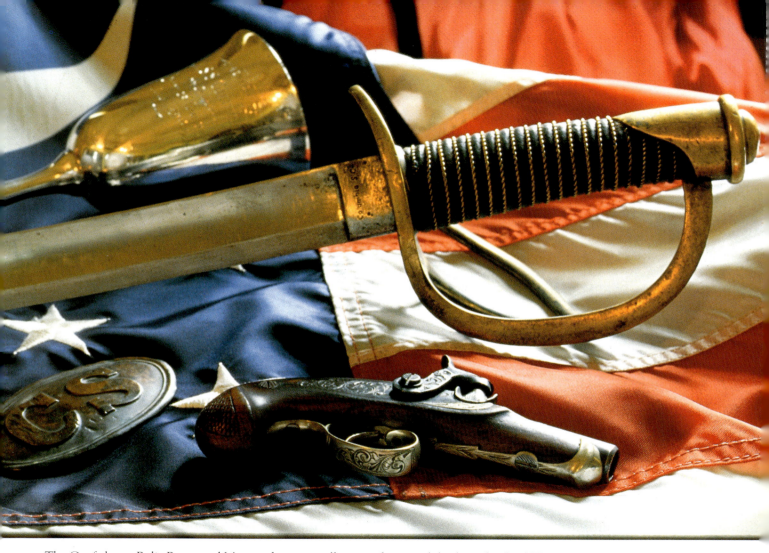

The Confederate Relic Room and Museum houses a collection of memorabilia from the Civil War and the Confederacy. Exhibits include weapons, uniforms, war memorabilia, women's fashions, Confederate stamps and monies printed in Columbia during the Civil War, and a variety of personal possessions of South Carolinians dating from the eighteenth century.

The South Caroliniana Library (built in 1840) was the first separate building erected on an American campus to house books. The large reading room is a replica of the Bullfinch's Congressional Library in the United States Capitol. The building has been attributed to the architect, Robert Mills.

The "Horseshoe" at the University of South Carolina. The university was chartered in 1805 as the South Carolina College. Within a few years the college had a student body of a hundred and a campus consisting of several graceful buildings surrounding a horseshoe-shaped green. The McKissick Museum houses art and science exhibits, The Baruch Silver Collection and a geological exhibit.

The President's House. The first president, Jonathan Maxcy, unable to secure professors in specific fields, shaped the curriculum to fit the abilities of the professors he could attract to Columbia. South Carolina College was best known as a training ground for orators. Maxcy is remembered by the Robert Mills monument in the center of the "Horseshoe".

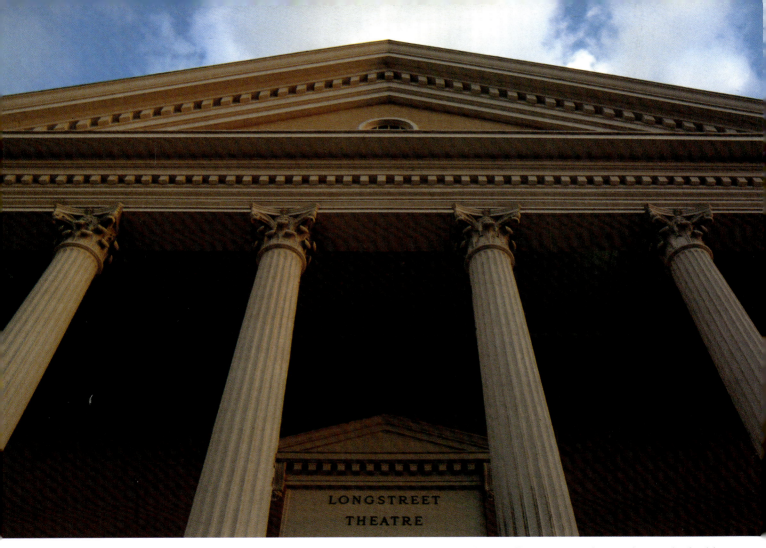

Longstreet Theatre was built in 1855 as a chapel and auditorium for South Carolina College. During the Civil War, the building was used first as an arsenal and then as a military hospital. Today it is a theater-in-the-round staging many University-sponsored performances.

First Presbyterian Church was built in 1854 in Gothic Revival style. Many of the churches and public buildings built in the middle of the 19th century have the tinted stucco exterior to imitate brownstone. Among Columbia's churches only the Presbyterian, Baptist and Episcopal churches survived from the antebellum days. The parents of President Wilson as well as his sister, Anne Howe, are buried in the churchyard.

The Columbia Museum of Art, South Carolina's largest fine art museum, emphasizes a broad spectrum of European and American fine and decorative arts dating from the 14th century to the present. The galleries are arranged in chronological order from Gallery 2 through Gallery 17. The museum offers a variety of temporary exhibitions, educational programs and special events.

The Columbia Museum of Art. Claude Monet, French 1840-1926. *L'Ile aux Orties, Giverny.*

The First Baptist Church. When Lincoln was elected president, the General Assembly called for a special convention to determine the state's future in the Union. The Secession Convention opened in Columbia on December 17, 1860, however, when smallpox broke out, it was decided to move the convention to Charleston. There on December 20, 1860, South Carolina voted unanimously to leave the Union.

The Seibels House was built shortly after the founding of Columbia in 1786 - the year "1796" can be seen carved on one of the basement beams. The house stands on plantation lands Thomas Taylor sold for about 8 dollars an acre and was part of the original two square miles. The Seibels family owned the house for over 130 years. The house is now owned by the Historic Columbia Foundation.

The Woodrow Wilson Boyhood Home was built by Reverend Joseph R. Wilson, the father of the 28th president. The Wilson family moved to Columbia in 1870 when Reverend Wilson joined the faculty of the Columbia Theological Seminary. Young Woodrow lived in Columbia for three years till he left for Davidson College. Furnished in the Victorian style, the house contains several Wilson family pieces.

Robert Mills House and Park is the former site of the Columbia Theological Seminary, founded 1828. The central building was designed by Robert Mills, Federal Architect of the United States, in 1823, as home for Columbia merchant, Ainsley Hall. When Hall died before the house was completed his widow was forced to sell. The seminary tore down the original outbuildings and built dormitories for students.

The Hampton-Preston Mansion was built in 1818 for Ainsley Hall. In 1823, Wade Hampton I purchased it as a townhome for his wife, Mary Cantey Hamptor. Their daughter, Caroline Hampton Preston and her husband, John S. Preston, a wealthy lawyer, planter, banker and politician made the house the center of Columbia's social life. The house is furnished with Hampton Preston family pieces.

Columbia's Churches. A sampling of the intricate architecture found among the numerous churches in Columbia.

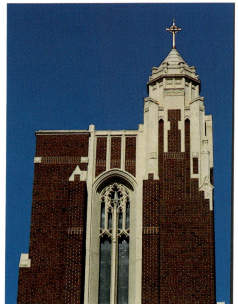
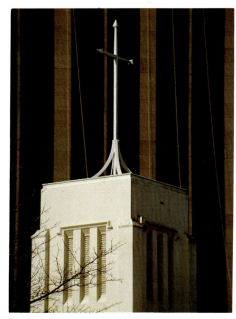
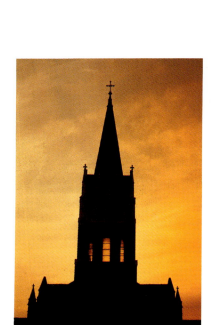

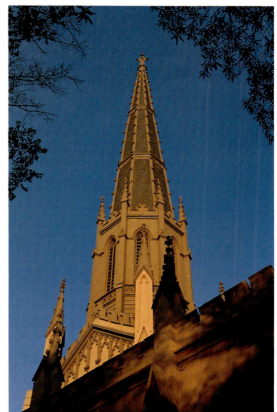

The Mann-Simons Cottage was the home of Celia Mann, a free African American in antebellum Columbia. According to family tradition, Celia Mann was born into slavery in Charleston in 1799. After acquiring her freedom, Celia Mann walked to Columbia and became a midwife. Her home became a center of the free African American community. The house remained in the Mann-Simons family for over 100 years.

The Caldwell-Boylston House located on the Governor's Green was built ca. 1830 and is known for its beautiful formal garden.

The Lace House (ca. 1855), located on the Governor's Green, was designed by a French architect from New Orleans.

The Governor's Mansion was built in 1855 to house officers of the Arsenal Academy. The Arsenal Academy was established to provide military training for young South Carolinians. By law, all white males had to belong to a militia unit whose main task was to help patrol the streets in lieu of a regular police force. Since 1868, the house has been the Governor's Mansion. Arsenal Hill is the highest point in Columbia.

Finlay Park. This 14-acre park in downtown Columbia boasts a waterfall and a lake. The park was the second step of the revitalization project *Congaree Vista*. Originally, named Sidney Park after the 19th-century park on the same site, it was renamed for former mayor, Kirk Finlay, who worked hard for the implementation of the ambitious plan to rejuvenate a 50-block area linking Main Street to the rivers.

Finlay Park. The plan for controlled growth of the downtown area goes back to Mayor Lester Bates who, in 1951, commissioned city planner C. A. Doxiadis to draw up a plan for Columbia's growth "looking 50 years into the future." The *Doxiadis Report* envisioned to link the underutilized river front to Main Street by cultural and recreational attractions, residential and commercial corridors and green spaces.

Riverbanks Zoological Park and Botanical Garden is a 170-acre park. Riverbanks Zoo houses more than 2,000 animals in natural habitat exhibits. Riverbanks Botanical Garden can be reached from the zoo via a footbridge and a half-mile long woodlands walk or by shuttle bus. The River Trail passes the ruins of the 19th-century Saluda Mill where hundreds of workers turned out cloth for the Confederacy.

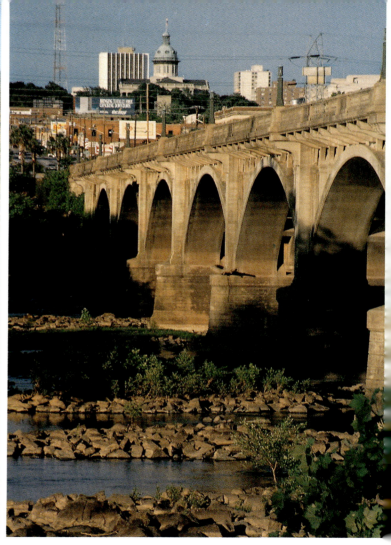

Congaree River.

 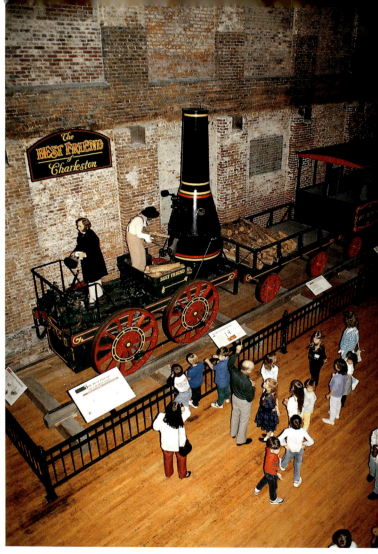

South Carolina State Museum is located in the historic Columbia Mill building, which opened in 1894 as the world's first totally electric textile mill. The exhibits inside the museum will give the visitor a comprehensive view of the Palmetto State - its art, history, natural history, science and technology from the first American-built locomotive to the suit worn on the moon by a South Carolina astronaut.

Gervais Street historic district is the heart of the Congaree Vista area.

Five Points, a popular area to dine.

Riverfront Park and the flood gates of the Columbia Canal.

The Columbia Canal was originally built so that river boats could skirt the rocks and rapids of the Congaree and move freight from the up-country to the low-country.

State Farmers Market

Williams-Brice Stadium

The Gamecocks

The Lights Before Christmas at Riverbanks Zoo & Garden

Ira and Nancy Koger Center For The Arts

Richland County Public Library

Sylvan's Jewelry. This building was built as a bank in 1871. It is Columbia's only Second Empire building. The four-faced sidewalk clock is a twin of one in Switzerland and was installed around 1908.

Baptist Medical Center

This statue of Wade Hampton III stands on the grounds of the State House. General Wade Hampton III (1818-1902), a wealthy planter and state senator, is believed to have been the largest landowner in South Carolina in 1860. In the spring of 1861, he organized Hampton's Legion. In 1876, Wade Hampton III became the first governor of South Carolina elected after Reconstruction.

Millwood was built for Wade Hampton II and his bride Ann FitzSimons in 1817. The plantation consisted of 12,000 acres on which Colonel Hampton was the first to plant other crops than cotton. However, his main interest was the breeding of his famous race horses. Millwood was burned to the ground by Union troops. The columns still stand on their original site off Garner's Ferry Road.

Fort Jackson was named after South Carolina-born president, Andrew Jackson. The U.S. Army Training Center at Fort Jackson was established in 1917 to prepare soldiers for WWI. Today, Fort Jackson is the Army's largest and most active initial training center. The Fort Jackson Museum covers more than 200 years of military history with emphasis on Fort Jackson's role of training and educating the new soldier.

Lake Murray

Congaree Swamp National Monument is a 22,000 acre alluvial flood plain located 20 miles southeast of Columbia off SC Route 48. Congaree Swamp is the last significant tract of old-growth bottomland hardwood forest in the U.S. and offers 18 miles of hiking trails, fishing, canoeing and camping. It also features two lakes and a boardwalk.

Camden, the oldest existing inland town in the state, was part of a township plan ordered by King George II in 1730. In 1758, Joseph Kernshaw established a store for a Charleston mercantile firm. During the Revolution, Lord Cornwallis and 2,500 British troops set up a supply post for the Southern Campaign. From 1780-81, the Kernshaw-Cornwallis House was used as headquarters for Lord Cornwallis.

Swan Lake Iris Garden near Sumter consists of 150 acres of Japanese irises, camellias, azaleas and magnolias surrounding a cypress bog. The black water of the bog reflects graceful swans and many shades of forest green. All eight species of the world's swans can be found here. The best time to view the irises is from May 15th to about June 20th. Azaleas, wisteria and dogwoods bloom from around March 20th to April 10th.

Edisto Memorial Gardens and Horne Wetlands Park, Orangeburg. This garden on the banks of the Edisto River is a mass of colorful azaleas, wisterias and other Southern favorites. The Horne Wetlands Park located within the garden takes visitors over a 2,300-foot boardwalk for a close-up look at the plants and wildlife found in the wetlands of this area. The adjacent Arts Center maintains a gallery on its second floor.

Boone Hall Plantation, Mount Pleasant, was a grant from the Lord Proprietors to Major John Boone, a member of Charles Towne's first settlers. This former cotton plantation has one of the most majestic avenues of moss-draped oaks in the South. Original plantation buildings include nine 18th-century slave cabins. In 1935, the original plantation was replaced with the present Georgian mansion.

Charleston, View of the Battery. Charleston was founded in 1670 by English settlers. Their adventure had been financed by eight Lord Proprietors who had been given the land stretching from North Carolina into Florida by King Charles II in gratitude for their help. Charleston became a wealthy export harbor first for indigo, then rice and cotton. It was the capital of South Carolina till 1786.

South Carolina Up-Country.

South Carolina Low-Country.

An aerial view of the South Carolina State House and Columbia.

BOOKS BY CITIES IN COLOR

CHARLESTON IN 88 PICTURES
SAVANNAH IN 88 PICTURES
NEW ORLEANS IN 88 PICTURES
SANTA FE IN 88 PICTURES
ATLANTA IN 88 PICTURES
GEORGIA IN 88 PICTURES

VIENNA, AUSTRIA
INNSBRUCK, AUSTRIA
SALZBURG, AUSTRIA
RIO DE JANEIRO, BRAZIL

CITIES IN COLOR, INC.
12 BRAEMORE DRIVE, NW
ATLANTA, GA 30328-4845
TEL.: 404-255-1054 FAX: 404-851-1940
E-MAIL: gmhoff@aol.com
www.citiesincolor.com

© CITIES IN COLOR, INC.